50
Simple Soups
for the Slow
Cooker

$6.99

4.95

Other Books by Lynn Alley

The Gourmet Slow Cooker
The Gourmet Slow Cooker: Volume II
The Gourmet Vegetarian Slow Cooker
The Gourmet Toaster Oven
Lost Arts: A Celebration of Culinary Traditions

50 Simple Soups for the Slow Cooker

Lynn Alley

**Andrews McMeel
Publishing, LLC**
Kansas City • Sydney • London

Andrews McMeel Publishing, LLC
an Andrews McMeel Universal company
1130 Walnut Street, Kansas City, Missouri 64106

www.andrewsmcmeel.com

11 12 13 14 15 LEO 10 9 8 7 6 5 4 3 2

ISBN: 978-1-4494-0793-3

Library of Congress Control Number: 2011921496

Photography: Ben Pieper
Food styling: Trina Kahl
Assistance: Dan Trefz

Attention: Schools and Businesses

Andrews McMeel books are available at quantity discounts with bulk purchase for educational, business, or sales promotional use. For information, please e-mail the Andrews McMeel Publishing Special Sales Department:
specialsales@amuniversal.com

To M, with love

Contents

Introduction

One of my favorite folktales is the beloved "Stone Soup" because it exemplifies just how easy it is to make a delicious soup out of almost nothing at all. A little rice, some tomatoes from the garden, a zucchini run amuck, some fresh spring herbs, some dried beans; anything and everything is fair game in a soup, whether one simple ingredient or a mélange of scavenged odds and ends.

From the proverbial *pot au feu*—bubbling away for days on the back of a French housewife's stove as scraps from each day's meals were tossed in, ensuring that nothing edible went to waste—to the creations that I whip up in my kitchen today using a slow cooker and an immersion blender, soups are a surefire way to make comfort, economy, and warmth pervade even the most humble of homes.

Soups are versatile, serving as everything from a first course, to a light lunch, to a hearty, stand-alone meal, to a dessert, and in some cases, even a breakfast. I remember my surprise at finding green salad and miso soup on the breakfast buffet at Honolulu's beautiful Halekulani Hotel, a traditional offering to the hotel's Japanese guests. Soups can be casual or formal, creamy or full of texture, light or heavier, hot or cold. They can be loaded with complex flavors and techniques, or made of one ingredient.

Easy on the Planet, the Palate, and the Pocketbook

I wanted to do a slow cooker soups book partly because I love soup so much and partly because I feel that many consumers today are looking for stuff that is easy to make, soul satisfying, and easy on the planet, the palate, and the pocketbook.

There can be no question that soup can be easy on the pocketbook. A great soup can often be put together using nothing more than a bag of beans and some good spices, or a few leftovers with some bright vegetables. And I can usually get several meals out of a good slow cooker full of soup, eating some now and freezing some for another day. A simple bowl of soup will fill a hungry belly for just a few pennies' worth of ingredients.

As for the planet, a good vegetable-based soup is far easier on the planet than is a juicy beef stew, for reasons that have been well exposed by a number of experts, beginning with Frances Moore Lappé in 1971 (*Diet for a Small Planet*) and John Robbins (*Diet for a New America*) in 1987. It takes a heck of a lot more resources to put a pound of flesh on a steer than it does to grow an acre of lima beans or corn. Latest statistics show that vast tracts of necessary-to-our-survival rain forests in South America have been cleared to feed America's burger habit, destroying not only our planet's "lungs" but also the way of life of many indigenous cultures. Add to this the fact that you can often rely upon farmers' markets for local produce, further reducing the impact on the planet's resources made by trucking ingredients over long distances.

The recipes in this book simply focus on fruits, grains, and vegetables, all of which offer a much greater array of colors, flavors, and textures than would meat, and all with minimal impact on the environment. When I taught cooking to middle school students many years ago, we talked about how meats basically have one color theme, and not a lot of variation in texture, whereas the plant kingdom offers reds, yellows, blues, purples, greens, and oranges, and all shades in between, and variations in texture that range from very soft like a banana, to hard like an apple, to the seeded insides of brightly colored pomegranates and passion fruits, to carrots and avocados, all kinder to the environment.

I don't mean to say that if you think you would enjoy one of the recipes more with some of last night's roast chicken, a leftover ham bone, or a bit of fresh shrimp, that you shouldn't be encouraged to add it. My neighbor Kathy, who eats every soup I make, sometimes adds chicken (which she loves to grill) to the soups to give her added protein. But I did want to demonstrate that a soup based upon vegetables only can be very rich in flavor and texture without relying upon canned chicken stock and chunks of meat or bone. Quite frankly, some of the best compliments I've received have come from people who were just sure you couldn't make a good soup without meat. What follows are some of the tricks I've used to infuse soups with rich flavors without meat.

Much has been written about the value of organic growing methods; however, I think most consumers miss one very important point: synthetic fertilizers and pesticides *were not created with your health in mind*. While they have enabled us to produce large quantities of food and feed a greater number of people worldwide, they have also contributed to destruction of the environment and created havoc with human and animal health.

This is not to say that many hardworking farmers would deliberately harm your health, but it *is* to say that your health is *not the farmer's bottom line*. Running his or her business is the bottom line. Keep this in mind and support those farmers who are willing to go the extra mile in the interests of keeping both you and the planet healthier for all concerned by using organic farming methods.

As for the palate (as well as other senses), I'll let the recipes speak for themselves.

Bang for Your Buck: Ways to Bump Up the Flavor

Professional chefs use a variety of cooking techniques to make the whole greater than the sum of its parts. Most of the soups in this book include a limited number of ingredients, but you can build flavor using some of these techniques.

One of the simplest ways to add flavor to a soup is to brown some or all of the ingredients before committing them to the pot. Onions can easily be chopped and added to the soup raw, but if you'd like to add an extra dimension of flavor, you can brown them in oil or butter first, anywhere from just softening them to giving them a nice golden hue. If you have a slow cooker with a cast aluminum insert suitable for use on the stovetop, then you won't even have to use an extra pan for browning.

Better still, brown the vegetables, then cook them in the slow cooker with a little oil *but no water* for anywhere from 2 to 6 hours before you add the water (see French Onion Soup, page 30). This method gives the vegetables an opportunity to further brown or caramelize, adding yet more flavor to your soup.

Salt is certainly a must-have in building the flavor of any good soup. Soup is one of those foods that cries out for plenty of salt and can taste very bland without it. Salt interferes with bitter taste receptors on your tongue; then you, as a result, taste the sweet or more desirable flavors in the soup instead of its bitter elements. Salt is a flavor enhancer for everything in the soup, not just a means of adding a salty taste.

You'll notice that I have left the matter of how much salt to add entirely to your taste; since we differ in our taste and tolerance for salt, it seems a good idea. A rule of thumb is to add about a tablespoon of salt to any one of the recipes in this book *as a starting point.* This is a starting point only. If the soup still tastes a little bland to you, try adding a little more salt, a little bit at a time, until you've reached optimum flavor. You'll be amazed at how *all* the flavors in the soup jump out at you with just a little additional salt.

I use Hain Pure Foods Sea Salt from my local health food store as my all-purpose cooking salt, but I enjoy, from time to time, using specialty salts, another great way to bump up the flavor of my soup. For example, I don't use smoked meats or fish, but I love a smoky flavor, so one of my favorite tricks is to use a good smoked salt. Specialty salt is rarely cheap, but it is one of the extravagances I allow myself from time to time because I enjoy it so much. Shop around. The last time I visited Dean & DeLuca in the Napa Valley, they had a hefty collection of specialty salts sold in bulk, including several types of smoked salt. Michael Chiarello's NapaStyle stores and catalog also offer a number of specialty salts packed in interesting and attractive boxes.

Special ingredients such as Maggi Seasoning sauce or Bragg Liquid Aminos can be an inexpensive way to add sodium and flavor to your soups and might be considered good replacements for ingredients such as beef or chicken stock. Maggi Seasoning sauce is a dark, hydrolyzed-vegetable protein-based sauce that is very similar to soy sauce but does not contain soy. It was originally developed in the 1880s as an easy way to improve the nutritional intake of German workers. Maggi is a staple seasoning in Germany, Austria, and Switzerland, and it can be purchased in many shops here in the United States. Bragg Liquid Aminos was developed by Dr. Paul Bragg in the 1930s as a seasoning with nutritional value. It is a nonfermented soy product, similar to soy sauce, that breaks down the soy proteins so that they are more bioavailable to the body.

Good, thrifty Italian cooks often add the hard rinds from Parmesan cheese to soups and sauces as they cook. The rinds are just the hardened surface of the cheese, so they will either puff up and get spongy (in which case you can fish them out of the soup before serving) or they will disintegrate into the soup. Either way, they give a wonderful flavor boost to soups. I keep a small plastic bag in the freezer for storing the rinds from Parmesan cheese until I need them. And at last check, my local Whole Foods store was actually selling the rinds of Parmigiano-Reggiano (the preeminent style of Parmesan cheese) as well as the cheese itself. Amounts are unspecified in those recipes that call for Parmesan rinds so that you can use what you have on hand. And in general, the more rinds, the more flavor!

When it comes to spices, I love to grind mine fresh just before adding them to a dish. This may sound formidable, but it is actually very easy and adds an extra dimension to your soups, since spices quickly lose their flavor when exposed to air, light, and heat. I buy spices from Penzeys, a wonderful online source for herbs and spices that has good prices, large volume, and rapid turnover, ensuring that your spices are flavorful and fresh. I store them in the freezer, then take out just the amount needed for any given recipe and grind it in a spice mill or electric coffee grinder just before using. It probably takes me no more than five minutes to gather spices and mill them for a recipe.

I also like to keep a healthy supply of fresh herb plants in my garden so that when I need a nip of rosemary, mint, thyme, or tarragon, I have only to step outside the kitchen door with a pair of scissors in hand. Fresh herbs I generally add at the last minute to retain their color, texture, and flavors.

Many of the recipes in this book call for ghee, or clarified butter. Because all of the milk solids have been removed, ghee can withstand cooking temperatures up to 485°F without smoking, so it is especially useful for sautéing and cooking. Buy it at any health food store or Indian market.

And last but not least, as any good lover of soups or stews knows, soup often tastes better the day after you make it. Somehow, the flavors seem to meld and gain depth when they sit overnight in the refrigerator. It's almost as if the dish, like a good wine, ripens over time.

A Word about Beans

Although many authors, experts, and cooks soak beans before cooking them, I never do. Soaking them may reduce your cooking time, and it may help rid the soup of the polysaccharides that give some individuals gas, but by and large, soaking beans is not necessary.

Bean cooking times may vary, sometimes greatly, in accordance with the condition of the beans themselves. Beans that have recently been harvested, for instance, are likely to be in good condition and will hydrate fairly quickly; beans that have been sitting on the shelf for a long time may take a very long time to cook (and occasionally, as in the case of very old beans, they may never fully become tender at all). The remedy? Try to purchase beans from a source with a rapid turnover rate, and check the package. If the beans look chipped or there are "crumbs" in the package, chances are the beans have been sitting around for a long time.

Indispensible Tools of the Trade

Slow Cooker

Choosing the right slow cooker is important. For several years, I have used and recommended the inexpensive slow cookers from Home Depot, Walmart, and Target. The big, fancy, very expensive digital models have always seemed superfluous to me. A digital panel is just one more thing that can break, and up until recently, I have been unable to discern any significant difference in the finished product or the ease of cooking between the cheap models and the more expensive ones.

That is to say until I *recently* found an expensive slow cooker that I enjoy very much: the All-Clad slow cooker with an anodized aluminum insert. The All-Clad insert can be used directly on top of the stove, so you can brown your ingredients, then lift the insert very carefully into the slow cooker casing so that you never have to use any other pans for your slow cooked meal. It is *very* easy to clean (unlike some cookware that claims to be easy to clean but really isn't). It has worked beautifully for me.

I keep several sizes of slow cooker on hand: a simple little Proctor Silex 1.5-quart oval slow cooker when I want to cook something for one or two people or melt small quantities of chocolate; a 3-quart round slow cooker for slightly larger quantities of soup, chili, polenta, or oatmeal, or for making fondue; a more conventional 5 or 6-quart oval model for cooking family-size meals that serve 4 to 6 people; and my favorite, the 7-quart All Clad with the anodized aluminum insert.

All recipes in this book were tested in the 7-quart slow cooker. *This means that if you are using a smaller slow cooker, your recipes may take a little longer to cook than the times recommended in the book.* The slow cooker is a very forgiving tool, and while you may have to watch closely at first to see how long the recipes take in your own slow cooker, the cooker times should be fairly accurate. I would caution you that different manufacturers and different sizes, however, can sometimes make a difference in cooking times, so keep your eye on the pot, and if something does not seem to be done by the time it should be (according to the recipe), just keep on cooking.

Handheld Immersion Blender

Here's a tool I wouldn't want to be without. Gone are the days when soup or sauce instructions read "puree in batches in your blender." I don't know about you, but I always managed to puree unevenly and slop stuff all over the kitchen counter. With a handheld immersion blender, pureeing a soup is but the work of a minute or two. You just hold the head of the blender underneath the surface of the soup (this is very important because if you let the head pop up above the surface, you'll splatter soup everywhere) and move it from spot to spot until the whole pot full of soup has been pureed to the texture you desire.

Spice Grinder

Many of the recipes in this book call for whole spices that are ground just before you use them on the principle that the spices will taste brighter and fresher if ground just before using, just like the pepper that is ground fresh over your salad at table. This may sound like a lot of work at first, but once you've got a system, the rest is easy. I nearly always buy spices whole and in bulk and store them in the freezer. When I want a little freshly ground cinnamon or a spice blend, I simply pull the spices out of the freezer and grind them up in an electric mill or by hand in a mortar and pestle. Either one works well. Within the last year, the ever-inventive folks at Cuisinart have come out with a spice and nut grinder made exclusively for this task. It has a heavy-duty stainless-steel blade designed especially for grinding spices and nuts, a dishwasher-safe bowl, and a plastic lid for storing spices in the bowl in case you grind more than you need. (I often store any leftover spice blends in clean baby food jars.) In addition, the booklet that comes with it has some great recipes in it: red chile powder, five-spice powder, chai (for tea), a curry blend, and a blend for pad thai noodles.

You could also use a coffee grinder devoted solely to spice grinding. I recommend using separate grinders for coffee and spices because the oils responsible for giving both coffee and spices their unique flavors and aromas will eventually leave residues in the grinder. So unless you enjoy the slight smell of cardamom or cumin in your coffee, devote a grinder to each purpose. When all else fails or if you are truly pressed for time, feel free to substitute commercially ground spices for the whole spices I've recommended in the recipes. Substituting 1 teaspoon of whole spice for 1 teaspoon of ground spice should get you close enough!

Preparing a Dish and Minimizing Your Work

Those of us who work a nine-to-five job rarely have time to do the prep work required for a soup before going to work in the morning. And while most of the recipes in this book require very little preparation other than browning onions, chopping vegetables, and grinding spices, all of these tasks can be done ahead of time to save stress and strain in the morning before you leave for work.

Ingredients can always be chopped up ahead of time and stored overnight in the refrigerator in plastic bags for easy assembly of a dish in the morning. Onions can even be browned and stored ahead of time, and spices can be ground and stored in plastic bags (or in a pinch, you can use already ground spices). Then in the morning, you can consign everything to the pot and turn it on before you walk out the door.

Cooking Times

You'll find that recipes in this book are fairly evenly divided among 4, 6, and 8-hour cooking times, with a slight emphasis on the 8-hour soups. It is my contention that while the 8-hour cooking time serves us on days when we must be away from home for long periods of time, there are also days when 4 hours with your hands free is just what you need. I, for instance, teach yoga classes, and I am rarely in a mood to cook when I return home after an evening class. I *can*, however, put something in the slow cooker before I go out to class and then come home to a hot soup or meal. I even wrote an article for the November 2010 issue of *Yoga Journal* on how to effectively use the slow cooker to support your yoga practice using a variety of cooking times!

Freezing Soups

One of the great joys of making a big pot of soup is that you often have leftovers to freeze. I frequently freeze individual portions of soup in small plastic containers or glass jars. It's great to be able to pull out an individual portion of soup when you're really hungry and too tired to cook. While many of the soups in this book freeze well, potato soups generally do not, so plan to consume them on the spot. And when freezing soups that require the addition of cream, milk, or cheese, try freezing the basic soup first, then adding the dairy only after the soup has been thawed and reheated.

Most soups should be good in the freezer for 4 to 6 months, tops, though I think using them within a month of freezing would be best. Reheating food in the slow cooker is *not* recommended because of food safety issues such as the possibility for bacterial growth. So, always reheat your soups in the microwave or on the stovetop.

Recipe Yield

In most cases, the recipes here are designed to yield 6 to 8 cups of soup. This should feed 4 to 6 people comfortably, depending upon the size of the serving. You will want a more generous serving of soup for a main course, for instance, than you will for a first course. And there is always the option of serving just a "taste" of soup to guests at a party as an appetizer, in which case a full recipe of soup will go a much longer way. In a couple of cases, as noted in the recipe, the recipe will serve more.

Adzuki Bean–Miso Soup

Serves 4 to 6

1 cup dried adzuki beans

6 cups water

⅓ cup mellow white miso

¼ pound firm tofu, cubed (optional)

¼ cup sliced scallions

Although we generally think of them as a favorite Japanese food, adzuki beans are believed to have been domesticated in the Himalayas several thousand years ago. By 1,000 B.C. they appeared in China, then later in Japan, where today they are second only to soybeans. They are small and cook quickly, and the tannins in their skins give the soup added color and flavor. This light soup is perfect for those occasions when you want to take the edge off the appetite without stuffing to the gills, or when you want a lot of broth with just a little bit of substance to it. You could also add some small cubes of tofu for extra protein.

Rinse the adzuki beans thoroughly, then place them in a 7-quart slow cooker along with the water and miso. Stir.

Cover and cook on LOW for about 4 hours, or until the beans are tender. Add the tofu and continue cooking for 15 minutes longer, or until the tofu is hot.

Ladle the soup into bowls. Top each bowl with the sliced scallions and serve.

Black Bean Chili with Cornbread Crust

Serves 6 to 8

Ahhh . . . I love this stuff. This is not your ordinary chili but reflects the rich combinations of ingredients found in real Mexican cuisine. You might even think of it as a bean mole, since it combines many of the spices and ingredients, including both chile powder and cocoa powder, usually found in mole poblano. It's got guts and flavor, and I love it with or without the cornbread crust. It's best sprinkled with lots of cheese, sliced olives, scallions, and cilantro.

Rinse the beans thoroughly and place them, along with the water, in a 7-quart slow cooker.

In a spice mill or mortar and pestle, grind the allspice, cinnamon, cumin, coriander, and aniseed. Add the spices, along with the tomatoes, onion, garlic, bell peppers, oregano, chile powder, and cocoa powder to the beans. Cover and cook on LOW for 6 to 8 hours, until the beans are tender.

Turn the slow cooker up to HIGH.

1 pound (2 cups) dried black beans

6 cups water

6 allspice berries

1 stick cinnamon

1 teaspoon cumin seed

1 teaspoon coriander seed

¼ teaspoon aniseed

1 (28-ounce) can crushed tomatoes

1 medium onion, diced

3 cloves garlic, finely minced

¼ cup diced red bell pepper

¼ cup diced green bell pepper

1 teaspoon dried Mexican oregano

1 to 2 tablespoons chile powder

¼ cup cocoa powder

To make the crust, in a food processor, pulse the cornmeal, flour, sugar, baking powder, baking soda, and salt until thoroughly mixed. Add the eggs, vegetable oil, and buttermilk and pulse until the liquid ingredients are thoroughly mixed in with the dry.

Spread the cornbread mixture over the top of the chili, or drop large spoonfuls around the surface of the chili, and continue cooking on HIGH with the lid slightly ajar for 1 hour longer, or until a toothpick inserted into the crust comes out clean.

Ladle the soup into bowls. Top each bowl with a dollop of sour cream and a sprinkling of scallions, olives, and cilantro.

Cornbread crust

1 cup cornmeal

1 cup all-purpose flour

¼ cup granulated sugar

1½ teaspoons baking powder

½ teaspoon baking soda

½ teaspoon salt

2 eggs

2 tablespoons vegetable oil

1 cup buttermilk

Toppings

½ cup sour cream or nonfat yogurt

¼ cup thinly sliced scallions

½ cup sliced black olives

½ cup chopped fresh cilantro

Avgolemono with Spinach and Dill

Serves 4 to 6

½ cup uncooked brown basmati or long-grain brown rice

6 cups water

1 medium onion, finely chopped

1 celery rib, diced

3 eggs

½ cup freshly squeezed lemon juice

1 tablespoon olive oil

4 ounces fresh spinach

Salt and freshly ground black pepper

¼ cup chopped fresh dill

Avgolemono is a traditional Greek chicken and lemon soup that rarely contains anything but chicken, lemon, eggs, and sometimes rice or onion. I know of few soups that are as redolent with the flavor of lemon—not just a hint, but a real serious draft of lemon. It requires more work than most of the recipes in this book but is well worth the extra effort. Avgolemono makes a great lunch, a first course, or a light supper in itself. The addition of spinach is mine, just for color and the flavor of spring. This is one soup that I would not attempt to reheat, as the egg is likely to curdle in a microwave or over a direct flame.

Rinse the rice thoroughly and place it, along with the water, onion, and celery in a 5 to 7-quart slow cooker. Stir.

Cover and cook on LOW for 4 to 5 hours, until the rice is tender.

Using a handheld mixer on medium speed, beat the eggs in a large bowl until quite frothy, then, with the mixer running, slowly drizzle in the lemon juice, followed by the olive oil.

Slowly add a ladle of broth, stirring constantly, to the lemon and egg mixture. If you hold a dipper or measuring cup full of broth above the mixing bowl and pour the broth in a slow, steady stream, you will avoid curdling the eggs.

Slowly add the lemon and broth mixture back into the soup, stirring constantly. Add the spinach and salt and pepper to taste. Let the soup stand until it begins to thicken, just a few minutes. If you allow the soup to boil or you let it stand for very long, the eggs will curdle.

Ladle the soup into bowls. Garnish with the chopped dill and serve immediately.

Black Bean Soup with Tomato, Cumin, and Coconut Milk

Serves 4 to 6

2 tablespoons ghee or vegetable oil (see page xv)

1 medium onion, finely chopped

2 cups dried black beans

6 cups water

1 cup crushed tomatoes

1 teaspoon cumin seed, lightly crushed

1 (15-ounce) can coconut milk or coconut cream

Salt

1 jalapeño pepper, seeded and thinly sliced

¼ cup chopped fresh cilantro leaves

Mention black bean soup to most Americans and they form a mental image that we all pretty much share: black beans, ham hocks, celery, carrots, onions, and thyme, or some variation on this theme. But here's a black bean soup with an Asian twist. The coconut milk adds a touch of sweetness and richness to the soup and makes it appeal to both kids and adults. Serve the soup as is, or puree the ingredients.

Heat the ghee in a sauté pan over medium heat and sauté the onion for about 10 minutes, or until lightly browned.

Rinse the beans thoroughly and add them, along with the water, onion, and tomatoes, to a 7-quart slow cooker.

Cover and cook on LOW for about 8 hours, or until the beans are tender.

Add the cumin seed, coconut milk, and salt to taste. Continue cooking for 30 to 60 minutes longer, until all the ingredients are hot.

Ladle the soup into bowls. Top each bowl with a couple of jalapeño slices and some cilantro.

Russian Borscht

Serves 4 to 6

Borscht, or some variation of it, has been a mainstay of peasant food all over eastern Europe and Russia. In the winter, the soup is served hot and may contain beets, carrots, and potatoes or other root vegetables; in the summer, the same soup (usually called chlodnik) may be served icy cold and mixed with cream, yogurt, or buttermilk and garnished with sliced radishes, beet greens, cucumbers, lemon slices, and hard-boiled eggs. Serve this soup hot or cold. Puree it or leave the vegetables whole. Eat it as you like it.

2 tablespoons butter or ghee (see page xv)

1 medium onion, chopped

3 pounds beets, peeled and cut into chunks

1 large potato, peeled and cut into cubes

1 large carrot, peeled and cut into 1-inch pieces

6 cups water

Salt

½ cup sour cream or Greek-style yogurt

¼ cup chopped fresh dill

In a large sauté pan, melt the butter over medium heat and sauté the onion for about 10 minutes, or until lightly browned.

Place the onion, beets, potato, carrot, and water in a 7-quart slow cooker. Cover and cook on LOW for about 6 hours, or until the beets are tender when pierced with a fork.

Using a handheld immersion blender, blend the vegetables until smooth. Add salt to taste.

Ladle the soup into bowls. Serve hot, garnished with sour cream and fresh dill.

Variation: For *chlodnik*, try mixing in 1 quart of plain yogurt and top with a small peeled, sliced cucumber and some chopped fresh dill, hard-boiled egg, and scallions.

Blue Cheese Potato Soup

Serves 4 to 6

2 tablespoons butter or ghee (see page xv)

1 medium onion, chopped

2 celery ribs, sliced

1½ pounds small red or white potatoes, skins on

6 cups water

8 ounces blue cheese (domestic, Roquefort, Gorgonzola, or your favorite)

4 cloves garlic

Salt

Freshly ground black pepper

Chopped fresh rosemary, for garnishing

My friend Julie and I were discussing the merits of slow cookers (she was about to spring big), and my findings with them. Funny how your ideas can become so much clearer when talking to a friend. "What I want to do is to show people that if they learn a few simple tricks about handling ingredients, they can turn out a delicious first-rate dish with a minimum of effort and without buying a bunch of exotic stuff that they'll never use again," I said. I love potatoes and just about any kind of cheese, and this soup is a perfect example of what I was talking about. The soup is made with a few simple ingredients, and you add flavor by sautéing the onion and celery and also by adding garlic. (Adding the garlic at the last minute retains its very pungent, garlicky flavor, which I like. If you prefer a milder garlic flavor, then add it along with the onions at the beginning of the cooking time.)

In a large sauté pan, melt the butter over medium heat and sauté the onion for about 10 minutes, or until lightly browned. Add the celery and cook for 2 minutes longer. Transfer the onion and celery to a 7-quart slow cooker and add the potatoes (but no water). Cover and cook on LOW for about 4 hours, or until the potatoes are very tender.

Add the water and blue cheese. Using a garlic press, mince the garlic into the soup. Add the salt to taste.

Using a handheld immersion blender, puree some of the ingredients to give the soup thickness and texture. For a more rustic feel, you can simply mash some of the potatoes with a potato masher. I like to leave it very lumpy and rustic looking with plenty of skin intact.

Ladle the soup into bowls. Grind the fresh pepper over the top and serve garnished with rosemary.

Cabbage Dal with Chile and Toasted Coconut

Serves 4 to 6

1 cup dried yellow lentils or split peas

6 cups water

1 medium onion, chopped

2 tablespoons ghee or vegetable oil (see page xv)

½ teaspoon black mustard seed

¼ teaspoon ground turmeric

¼ pound napa cabbage, shredded

Salt

Basmati rice, for serving (optional)

1 tablespoon shredded coconut, toasted

1 serrano chile, seeded and thinly sliced

For several years, I worked as a yoga instructor at the Chopra Center for Wellbeing in Southern California. As a part of their Perfect Health program, a young Indian woman prepared a different dal, the classic ayurvedic dish for internal cleansing, each day. If I close my eyes, I can still smell and even taste Aparna's wonderful dal, all of which started me on a quest of my own for the perfect dal recipe.

Rinse the lentils thoroughly, then place them in a 7-quart slow cooker. Add the water and half the onion. Cover and cook on LOW for 4 to 5 hours, until the lentils are quite tender. At this point, you can mash some of the lentils to give the soup a thicker consistency.

In a large sauté pan, melt the ghee over medium heat and sauté the remaining onion for about 10 minutes, or until lightly browned. Add the mustard seed and cook for 1 to 2 minutes longer.

About 10 minutes before serving, add the onion and mustard seed, the turmeric, and cabbage and stir. Add the salt to taste.

Serve either in a soup bowl or ladled over the basmati rice. Top with the shredded coconut and chile.

Cauliflower, Stilton, and Fines Herbes Soup

Serves 4 to 6

A more truly British soup would be hard to find. You could even include some good cheddar in addition to the Stilton.

In a large sauté pan, melt the butter over medium heat and sauté the onion for about 10 minutes, or until lightly browned. Add the celery and cook for 2 to 3 minutes longer.

Transfer the onion and celery to a 7-quart slow cooker and add the cauliflower and water. Cover and cook on LOW for about 4 hours, or until the cauliflower is nice and tender.

Using a handheld immersion blender, puree the ingredients until smooth. Stir in ½ cup of the Stilton, the cheddar, and half-and-half. Add the salt to taste.

Ladle the soup into bowls. Garnish each bowl with the remaining Stilton and some of the herbs just before serving.

Note: For more flavor, you can substitute ½ cup dry white wine for ½ cup water.

2 tablespoons butter or ghee (see page xv)

1 medium onion, chopped

2 celery ribs, finely chopped

1 large cauliflower, coarsely chopped

5 cups water (see Note)

1 cup crumbled Stilton or other blue cheese, divided

½ cup grated sharp cheddar cheese

1 cup half-and-half

Salt

¼ cup chopped fresh herbs, such as chives, parsley, tarragon, and/or chervil

Chickpea Soup Arrabbiata

Serves 6 to 8

2 tablespoons olive oil

1 medium onion, chopped

1 pound (2 cups) dried chickpeas

2 medium carrots, peeled and diced

2 celery ribs, diced

1 (28-ounce) can crushed tomatoes

1 (6-ounce) can tomato paste

7 cups water

1 teaspoon chile flakes

2 bay leaves

1 Parmesan cheese rind, or more if desired

2 teaspoons chopped fresh oregano

2 teaspoons fresh thyme leaves

4 cloves garlic, or more

Salt

¼ cup chopped fresh parsley

2 tablespoons basil chiffonade (see Note)

Chickpeas, or ceci as they are called in Italian, are found widely in the cucina povera (or peasant cuisine) of Italy and most countries of the Mediterranean region. This soup is especially good if you have saved some Parmesan cheese rinds and can add them to the soup as it cooks. I like to press in garlic at the last minute to maximize its strength and flavor.

In a large sauté pan, heat the olive oil over medium heat and sauté the onion for about 10 minutes, or until lightly browned.

Rinse the chickpeas thoroughly and place them in a 7-quart slow cooker. Add the onion, carrots, celery, tomatoes, tomato paste, water, chile flakes, bay leaves, and Parmesan rind. Cover and cook on LOW for about 8 hours, or until the chickpeas are tender.

Add the oregano and thyme. Using a garlic press, mince the garlic into the soup, then add the salt to taste. Using a handheld immersion blender, puree some of the mixture to thicken the soup. (I usually puree about one-quarter of the soup.)

Ladle the soup into bowls. Serve each bowl garnished with parsley and basil.

Note: To make the chiffonade, stack the basil leaves, roll them up lengthwise, then slice thinly across the roll.

Celery Root Soup

Serves 4 to 6

2 tablespoons butter or
   ghee (see page xv)

3 medium leeks, sliced
   (white and pale green
   parts only)

1½ pounds celery root,
   peeled and cut into
   1-inch pieces

5 cups water

1 cup half-and-half or soy
   cream (optional)

Salt

1 Granny Smith apple,
   unpeeled, cut into
   matchsticks

1 celery rib, thinly sliced

⅓ cup inner celery leaves

For centuries, root vegetables like potatoes, turnips, carrots, and rutabagas were the dietary mainstay of people throughout northern Europe during the winter when more fragile crops that grew aboveground were unobtainable. The celery root (also known as celeriac or the turnip-rooted celery), though not as widely accepted as the potato, can be found in salads and soups during the colder months of the year. It is easy to clean (peel it like you would a potato) and offers the same pleasant flavor and aroma of its stalky, leafy cousin.

In a large sauté pan, melt the butter over medium heat and sauté the leeks for about 10 minutes, or until lightly browned.

Transfer the leeks to a 7-quart slow cooker and add the celery root and water. Cover and cook on LOW for 4 to 6 hours, until the celery root is tender.

Add the half-and-half, then using a handheld immersion blender, puree the soup. Add the salt to taste. Cook for about 30 minutes longer, or until all the ingredients are hot.

Ladle the soup into bowls and top each bowl with a bit of apple, sliced celery rib, and celery leaves.

Creamy Butternut Squash, Mushroom, Prune, and Rice Soup

Serves 4 to 6

It's an odd combination, admittedly, but I got this idea from a friend who once served skewers of prune and butternut squash grilled over an open fire at a backyard dinner party. I loved the flavors and decided to try them in a soup, accented with fresh tarragon. The results won the approval of my neighborhood taste testers, hands down.

In a large sauté pan, heat the olive oil over medium heat and sauté the onion for about 10 minutes, or until lightly browned.

Transfer the onion to a 7-quart slow cooker and add the celery, squash, mushrooms, rice, prunes, and water. Cover and cook on LOW for 4 to 6 hours, until the squash is quite tender and the rice is done.

Add the salt to taste and stir in the tarragon and parsley. Ladle into bowls and serve immediately.

2 tablespoons olive oil

1 medium onion, finely chopped

1 celery rib with leaves, finely chopped

1 small butternut squash, peeled and cubed

1 ounce dried mushrooms

½ cup uncooked Arborio rice

1 cup pitted prunes, coarsely chopped

6 cups water

Salt

1 tablespoon chopped fresh tarragon

1 tablespoon chopped fresh parsley

Corn Chowder with Potatoes, Poblanos, and Smoked Gouda

Serves 4 to 6

4 tablespoons butter or
   ghee (see page xv)

1 medium onion, chopped

1 pound small potatoes,
   sliced

1 bay leaf

4 sprigs fresh thyme

6 cups water

4 cups fresh or frozen corn

2 poblano chiles, roasted,
   peeled, and diced, or
   1 (4-ounce) can diced
   roasted chiles

1 cup half-and-half

1 cup grated smoked
   cheddar or Gouda
   cheese, divided

Salt (preferably smoked)

¼ cup grated smoked
   cheddar or Gouda cheese

Chopped chives, for
   garnishing

Because corn chowder is usually made with smoked bacon, I like to add smoked salt and a smoked Gouda to this soup instead. If the potatoes are organic (and I hope they are; you don't want to know what kind of heinous fumigants are used on conventionally farmed potatoes), leave the skins on them for extra flavor and a more rustic feel.

In a large sauté pan, melt the butter over medium heat and sauté the onion for about 10 minutes, or until lightly browned.

Transfer the onion to a 7-quart slow cooker and add the potatoes, bay leaf, thyme, and water. Cover and cook on LOW for about 4 hours, or until the potatoes are tender.

Mash some of the potatoes against the inside of the cooker or use a handheld immersion blender to puree a small amount of potato and thicken the soup slightly.

Add the corn, chiles, half-and-half, and ¾ cup of the cheddar. Add the salt to taste and continue cooking for 20 to 30 minutes, or just until all the ingredients are hot.

Ladle the soup into bowls and garnish each bowl with the remaining cheddar and chopped chives.

Countrywild Rice Soup

Serves 4 to 6

⅔ cup uncooked Lundberg Countrywild rice

1 ounce dried mushrooms

3 tablespoons olive oil

1 medium onion, chopped

4 cloves garlic, sliced

½ cup diced carrots

½ cup diced celery

1 bay leaf

Parmesan cheese rind

6 cups water

1 cup cream or half-and-half (optional)

½ cup fresh or frozen peas

¼ cup chopped fresh tarragon or parsley

1 tablespoon Maggi Seasoning sauce or Bragg Liquid Aminos (see page xiv)

Salt and freshly ground black pepper

½ cup freshly grated Parmesan cheese

Albert and Frances Lundberg, having seen the ravages of poor, shortsighted farming methods on the land of Nebraska in the Depression-era Dust Bowl, moved their family to California's Sacramento Valley in 1937 and planted rice. They impressed upon their sons the great importance of caring for the soil and went on to pioneer organic rice growing in America, going so far as to develop some of their own unique varieties of aromatic rice. I have enjoyed experimenting with their high-quality traditional rice such as basmati, Arborio, and classic brown, as well as some more unusual varieties, such as their Black Japonica and red Wehani. This recipe calls for my favorite: Countrywild, a blend of Wehani, brown rice, and Black Japonica. The soup has a fairly mild flavor and really depends upon the addition of the freshly grated Parmesan cheese for character and oomph.

Thoroughly rinse the rice and the mushrooms in separate containers and set them aside.

In a large sauté pan, heat the olive oil over medium heat and sauté the onion for about 10 minutes, or until lightly browned. Add the garlic and rice and cook for 3 minutes longer.

Transfer the mixture to a 7-quart slow cooker and add the mushrooms, carrots, celery, bay leaf, Parmesan rind, and water. Cover and cook on LOW for about 6 hours, or until the rice is quite tender.

Stir in the cream, peas, 2 tablespoons of the tarragon, and the seasoning sauce and continue to cook for 30 minutes longer, until hot. Stir in the salt and pepper to taste.

Ladle the soup into bowls and serve topped with some freshly grated Parmesan cheese and the remaining 2 tablespoons of tarragon.

Cream of Artichoke Soup

Serves 4 to 6

3 tablespoons olive oil

1 medium onion, chopped

4 cloves garlic

1 pound small Yukon gold potatoes

4 large artichokes (about 1½ pounds) (see Note)

6 cups water

¼ cup freshly squeezed lemon juice

Salt

¼ cup chopped fresh tarragon, chervil, or parsley (or a combination)

I've made great artichoke soups with frozen artichoke hearts and with canned artichoke hearts. Both have been easy and satisfying. But as the first flowers of spring are emerging after a wonderful, rainy winter, and artichokes are making their appearance in the produce markets, I want to make a soup with the real deal: fresh artichokes. Medium-size mature artichokes can easily stand 4 to 6 hours of cooking and yield a soup of more interesting texture and flavor than soups from frozen or canned varieties.

In a large sauté pan, heat the olive oil over medium heat and sauté the onion for about 10 minutes, or until lightly browned. Add the garlic and sauté for 1 to 2 minutes longer.

Transfer the mixture to a 7-quart slow cooker and add the potatoes, artichokes, and water. Cover and cook on LOW for 4 to 6 hours, until the artichokes are very tender.

Using a handheld immersion blender, puree the ingredients. Add the lemon juice and salt to taste. Additional water may be needed; add it to achieve the texture and thickness you desire.

Ladle the soup into bowls and top each serving with a sprinkling of herbs.

Note: Contrary to what you might imagine, preparing the artichokes isn't all that difficult. Just snap off the tough outer leaves until you get down to the creamy, softer leaves, and cut off the tops of the artichokes, leaving about 1 inch of leaf. Then cut the artichokes into quarters and scoop out their centers (all the fuzzy and prickly stuff) and drop them into the slow cooker with water in it. And in this case, the "cream" in the soup is supplied by potatoes!

Garlic, Onion, and Leek Soup with Cream

Serves 4 to 6

2 tablespoons olive oil

4 heads garlic, cloves separated and peeled

1 medium onion, sliced

2 leeks, thinly sliced (white and pale green parts only)

4 tablespoons all-purpose flour

6 cups water

1 cup half-and-half

1 tablespoon freshly squeezed lemon juice

⅓ cup dry sherry

Salt

¼ cup freshly grated Parmesan cheese, for garnishing

Chopped chives, for garnishing

I've always enjoyed garlic, so much that I once went to the Gilroy Garlic Festival just to see what all the fuss was about. I ate garlic ice cream and garlic-filled chocolates and garlic chocolate chip cookies. So I guess I would never write a soup book without at least one or two garlic soup recipes. This one is quite mild and creamy.

Place the olive oil, garlic, onion, and leeks in a 7-quart slow cooker (without any water). Cover and cook on LOW for about 4 hours, or until the onion and garlic are golden.

Sprinkle the flour evenly over the onion, add the water, and stir. Cover and cook on LOW for 4 hours longer, or until the leeks are tender.

Add the half-and-half, and using a handheld immersion blender, puree some of the ingredients to the texture you desire. Stir in the lemon juice and sherry, and add the salt to taste.

Ladle the soup into bowls. Garnish each bowl with Parmesan cheese and chives.

Indian Dried Mushroom Soup

Serves 4 to 6

Somehow when I think of mushroom soups and stews, I think of France and northern Italy. But this is silly. Mushrooms of one type or another grow all over the world, and they regularly turn up in the cuisine of nearly every country on earth. India is no exception, yet few of us have experienced a good Indian meal involving mushrooms. This may be a first for you, just as it once was for me.

In a large sauté pan, heat the vegetable oil over medium heat and sauté the onion for about 10 minutes, or until lightly browned.

Rinse the mushrooms thoroughly and place them, along with the onion, carrots, tomatoes, and water in a 7-quart slow cooker. Cover and cook on low for about 6 hours.

Grind the cumin, fennel, coriander, cardamom, cloves, and peppercorns and add them to the soup. Continue cooking for 30 minutes longer. Add the salt to taste.

Ladle the soup into bowls and garnish each with a dollop of yogurt and a sprinkling of chile and cilantro.

2 tablespoons vegetable oil

1 medium onion, sliced into 8 pieces from pole to pole

1 ounce dried mushrooms

3 medium carrots, peeled and sliced

2 large tomatoes, coarsely chopped

6 cups water

1 teaspoon cumin seed

½ teaspoon fennel seed

1 tablespoon coriander seed

Seeds from 3 cardamom pods

6 cloves

½ teaspoon black peppercorns

Salt

½ cup Greek-style yogurt

1 serrano chile, seeded, deveined, and finely chopped

¼ cup chopped fresh cilantro

Cuban Black Bean and Sweet Potato Soup

Serves 4 to 6

2 tablespoons olive oil

1 medium onion, diced

1 cup diced celery

1 cup diced carrots

1 cup chopped tomatoes

1 cup dried black beans

6 cups water

1 medium sweet potato, peeled and cut into ½-inch cubes

1 medium green bell pepper, seeded and diced

2 teaspoons ground cumin

1 bay leaf

1 teaspoon dried Mexican oregano

1 teaspoon ground cinnamon

3 cloves garlic

Pinch of chile flakes

Salt

2 jalapeño chiles, seeded and thinly sliced

½ avocado, diced

Cuban culinary traditions reflect the Spanish, African, and Caribbean roots of the island's population. Beans and rice, as in most Spanish-rooted cultures, are popular. And in Cuba, some kind of root vegetable is often added to the meal. Traditionally, this colorful, hearty soup can be made with pork bones or meat, but the same soup without the oinker is cheaper and even more true to its ingredient flavors and colors. This recipe yields a very thick soup, so add water if you'd like a thinner version. If you're pressed for time, you could put all the ingredients in at one time, but adding the sweet potato after the beans are mostly cooked helps to preserve its texture and color.

In a large sauté pan, heat the olive oil over medium heat and sauté the onion for about 10 minutes, or until lightly browned. Add the celery and carrots and cook for 2 minutes longer.

Transfer the mixture to a 7-quart slow cooker and add the tomatoes, black beans, and water. Cover and cook on LOW for about 6 hours.

Add the sweet potato, bell pepper, cumin, bay leaf, oregano, and cinnamon and continue to cook on LOW for 2 to 3 hours longer, until the beans and sweet potato are quite tender.

Using a garlic press, mince the garlic into the soup. Add the chile flakes and salt to taste.

Ladle the soup into bowls and garnish each with jalapeños and avocado.

Eggplant Soup
with Cumin, Yogurt, and Dill

Serves 4 to 6

Eggplant is the base for baba ghanoush. Some kind of pureed eggplant appetizer is a staple in most Middle Eastern and Mediterranean cuisines. And since everybody likes it, why not turn it into a soup and serve it with toasted pita triangles?

In a large sauté pan, heat the olive oil over medium heat and sauté the onion for about 10 minutes, or until lightly browned.

Transfer the onion to a 7-quart slow cooker and add the eggplant and water. Cover and cook on LOW for 4 to 6 hours, until the eggplant is very tender.

Using a garlic press, mince the garlic into the soup, then puree the soup using a handheld immersion blender. Coarsely grind the cumin seed and add it to the soup. Add the salt and pepper to taste.

Ladle the soup into bowls. Mix together the yogurt and dill and top each bowl with a tablespoon or two.

3 tablespoons olive oil

1 medium onion, coarsely chopped

1 large eggplant, peeled and cut into chunks

5 cups water

3 cloves garlic

2 teaspoons cumin seed, coarsely ground

Salt and freshly ground black pepper

½ cup Greek-style yogurt or sour cream

¼ cup chopped fresh dill or cilantro

French Onion Soup

Serves 4 to 6

3 tablespoons unsalted
   butter

6 large onions, either
   sliced or halved and
   cut from pole to pole into
   ¼-inch-thick slices

3 cloves garlic, sliced

1 bay leaf

6 sprigs fresh thyme

½ cup dry sherry

6 cups water

Salt

Freshly ground black
   pepper

4 to 6 slices of baguette,
   ½ inch thick

8 ounces shredded Gruyère
   cheese

Recently my neighbor Kathy made a French onion soup that called for roasting onions in the oven for several hours to develop flavor before making the soup itself. It seemed like too much work to her, so she scrapped the idea. I thought it was a great idea, but why not do the whole thing in the slow cooker? What an easy task: onions, slow cooked for hours in nothing but a bit of butter, become dark, rich, and full of flavor.

Place the butter, onions, and garlic in the slow cooker (without the water). Cover and cook, stirring once or twice, on HIGH for 6 to 8 hours, until the onions are nice and brown and very tender.

Turn the heat down to LOW. Add the bay leaf, thyme, sherry, and water and salt to taste. Cover and cook for 2 hours longer.

Preheat the broiler. Grind some fresh pepper into the soup, then ladle the soup into ovenproof bowls. Top each bowl with a slice or two of baguette and sprinkle with cheese. Place the bowls on a baking sheet positioned about 6 inches under the broiler and broil until the cheese is bubbly and melted. If you do not have ovenproof bowls, the soup is just as good with the cheese simply sprinkled on the top. It just won't have that nice, golden crust.

Garnet Yam Soup with Coconut Cream

Serves 4 to 6

This fits my "good soup" requisites: made with a few simple ingredients, packed with flavor, and easy to make. Coconut cream and cilantro give the soup an Asian flair, and the rich, reddish orange soup with bright green peas makes a beautiful visual presentation.

In a large sauté pan, melt the butter over medium heat and sauté the onion for about 10 minutes, or until lightly browned.

Transfer the onion to a 7-quart slow cooker and add the yams (without the water). Cover and cook on LOW for about 4 hours, or until the vegetables are soft and somewhat caramelized.

Add the coconut cream and water. Using a handheld immersion blender, puree the ingredients to the desired texture. I like to leave a few chunks in the soup. Cook for 1 to 2 hours longer, until all the ingredients are uniformly hot.

Stir in the peas, add the salt to taste, and cook for 20 to 30 minutes longer.

Ladle the soup into bowls. Top each bowl with a sprig of cilantro and serve.

2 tablespoons butter or ghee (see page xv)

1 medium onion, sliced

3 garnet (red) yams, peeled and cut into chunks

1 (15-ounce) can coconut cream

5 cups water

2 cups fresh or frozen peas

Salt

4 to 6 sprigs fresh cilantro

Enchilada Soup

Serves 4 to 6

6 dried California or New Mexico chiles

7 cups water, divided

1 tablespoon vegetable oil

1 medium onion, chopped

4 cloves garlic, minced

⅓ cup dried pinto beans

4 large tomatoes, coarsely chopped

1 teaspoon cumin seed

2 teaspoons dried Mexican oregano

Salt

1 cup tortilla chips made from stone-ground cornmeal

1 cup grated sharp cheddar cheese or smoked Gouda

½ cup sliced black California olives

½ cup sliced scallions

¼ cup chopped fresh cilantro

½ cup sour cream

My grandfather was a big enchilada man—he even made his own sauce from scratch. He learned it from the cooks on the ranch where he grew up and passed his recipe on to mom and me. Enchiladas and beans taste like home to me, so I loved the idea of this soup. It's so delish, and I can almost see gramps smiling down from heaven.

Remove the seeds, stems, and veins from the chiles, then tear them into pieces. Soak them in 1 cup of the water for 2 hours or overnight.

In a large sauté pan, heat the vegetable oil over medium heat and sauté the onion for about 10 minutes, or until lightly browned. Add the garlic and cook for 2 minutes longer.

Rinse the pinto beans and place them in the slow cooker, along with the onion and garlic, the tomatoes, and the remaining water. Puree the soaked chiles and water in a blender and pour the sauce into the slow cooker. Cover and cook on LOW for about 8 hours, or until the beans are tender. Add the cumin and oregano about 1 hour before serving. Add the salt to taste.

Ladle the soup into bowls. Top each bowl with tortilla chips, cheese, olives, scallions, cilantro, and sour cream.

Hot and Sour Soup

Serves 4 to 6

5 cups water

1 ounce dried shiitake mushrooms

1 tablespoon grated fresh ginger

1 teaspoon granulated sugar

2 tablespoons rice vinegar, or more

¼ cup tamari

1 (6-ounce) can water chestnuts

¼ teaspoon chile flakes

½ cup fresh or frozen peas

6 ounces firm tofu, diced

Toasted sesame oil

2 scallions, sliced

This simple recipe for hot and sour soup is the perfect choice for a cold day or an oncoming flu. It can be put together in a matter of minutes from ingredients you probably already have on hand. Although hot and sour soups typically contain bamboo shoots, I don't like the canned variety, so I've substituted water chestnuts, which have a nice crunch to them. You can also drizzle in a lightly beaten egg at the very end of cooking if you so desire.

Place the water, mushrooms, ginger, sugar, rice vinegar, and tamari in a 7-quart slow cooker. Cover and cook on LOW for about 4 hours.

Just before serving, add the water chestnuts, chile flakes, peas, tofu, and sesame oil to taste.

Ladle the soup into bowls. Garnish each with scallions.

Kashmiri Black Bean Soup

Serves 6 to 8

When most of us think of Indian food, we think of lentils or chickpeas as the legumes of choice. But most Indians are vegetarian, and since legumes are a primary source of protein for them, the array of beans that actually appears on the table in India is far more expansive than we imagine. This Kashmiri recipe uses black beans similar to the kind we use here in Mexican, Cuban, and southwestern dishes. I've also made this dish with pink beans with equally savory results. It's a simple dish with the typical seasonings of the Indian subcontinent.

2 cups (1 pound) dried black, pink, or kidney beans

6 cups water

2 teaspoons fennel seed

2 teaspoons ground turmeric

1 teaspoon ground ginger

1 teaspoon garam masala or curry powder

½ teaspoon chile flakes (optional)

Salt

¼ cup coarsely chopped fresh cilantro

Rinse the beans thoroughly, then place them in a 7-quart slow cooker with the water. Cover and cook on LOW for about 8 hours, or until the beans are tender.

Using a handheld immersion blender, puree the beans to the desired texture. I like to leave some large pieces.

Coarsely grind the fennel seed, then add them to the beans. Stir in the turmeric, ginger, garam masala, and chile flakes. Add the salt to taste.

Ladle the soup into bowls and garnish each with a sprinkle of cilantro.

Hummus Soup with Kalamata Olives and Mint

Serves 4 to 6

1 cup dried chickpeas (garbanzo beans)

6 cups water

1 teaspoon cumin seed

1 teaspoon coriander seed

2 tablespoons tahini

2 to 3 tablespoons freshly squeezed lemon juice

3 cloves garlic, or more

½ cup Greek-style yogurt

¼ cup chopped kalamata olives

¼ cup chopped fresh parsley or mint

Like baba ghanoush, some variation on hummus is found in most Mediterranean and Middle Eastern countries. Why not turn the same humble ingredients into a soup? And if you like, add artichoke hearts, slivered black olives, or roasted red peppers, which are sometimes added to hummus in America. Greek country salad and fresh, hot pita would make a nice accompaniment.

Rinse the chickpeas thoroughly and place them in a 7-quart slow cooker along with the water. Cover and cook on LOW for 6 to 8 hours, until the chickpeas are tender.

Coarsely grind the cumin and coriander seeds and add them and the tahini and lemon juice to the chickpeas. Use a garlic press to mince the garlic into the soup. Using a handheld immersion blender, puree the chickpeas to the desired consistency.

Ladle the soup into bowls. Top each with yogurt, olives, and parsley.

Curried Butternut Squash Soup

Serves 4 to 6

2 tablespoons butter or ghee (see page xv)

1 medium onion, coarsely chopped

1 medium butternut squash, peeled and cut into 1½-inch chunks

5 cups water

2 teaspoons curry powder or garam masala

1 teaspoon chile powder

1 cup coconut cream

Salt

2 tablespoons coarsely chopped fresh cilantro

¼ cup roasted pumpkin seeds, chopped

¼ cup Greek-style yogurt (optional)

My first brush with Indian food came at the hands of a Sikh family who had come from Punjab to watch over their two kids at the University of California. They had opened a small restaurant in Berkeley where the mother plied her home cooking and the father ran the front of the house. The food was humble, yet delicious in a way that only home cooking can be.

In a large sauté pan, melt the butter over medium heat and sauté the onion for about 10 minutes, or until lightly browned.

Transfer the onion to a 7-quart slow cooker and add the squash (without the water). Cover and cook on LOW for about 2 hours, or until the squash is tender.

Add the water, curry powder, and chile powder and cook on LOW for 2 to 4 hours longer.

Using a handheld immersion blender, puree the contents of the slow cooker until it reaches the desired consistency. Stir in the coconut cream and add the salt to taste.

Ladle the soup into bowls and garnish each with cilantro, pumpkin seeds, and a dollop of yogurt.

Korean-Style Black Bean Soup

Serves 6 to 8

I love black beans, but most black bean soup recipes are fairly predictable: beans, carrots, celery, maybe some thyme, maybe a ham hock. I wanted a black bean soup that's a little different, so I took an Eastern approach, adding soy sauce and ginger. It is important to use low-sodium soy sauce, since full sodium is likely to be overwhelming.

In a large sauté pan, heat the vegetable oil and sauté the onion for about 10 minutes, or until lightly browned. Add the garlic and ginger and cook for 2 minutes longer.

Transfer the mixture to a 7-quart slow cooker and add the beans, water, soy sauce, and honey. Cover and cook on LOW for 6 to 8 hours, until the beans are tender.

Using a handheld immersion blender, puree the beans. Stir in the sesame oil. Check the seasoning and add the salt if needed.

Ladle the soup into bowls and garnish each with scallions and sesame seed.

2 tablespoons vegetable oil

½ medium onion, coarsely chopped

6 cloves garlic, peeled

1-inch piece fresh ginger, peeled and minced

2 cups dried black beans, rinsed thoroughly

8 cups water

⅓ cup low-sodium soy sauce

1 tablespoon honey

2 tablespoons toasted sesame oil

Salt (optional)

2 tablespoons sliced scallions (green parts only)

4 teaspoons toasted sesame seed

Indian Spiced Fresh Tomato Soup

Serves 4 to 6

At a motel in Davis, California, I noticed that beans, eggplants, peas, tomatoes, basil, and cilantro had been planted around an outbuilding. Suspecting the handiwork of some Italian gardener, I was surprised one morning to discover an elderly lady dressed in a lovely sari tending the garden. She was the proprietor's mother. Wonderful and very unique dishes can be created using the same ingredients, just in different parts of the world with slightly different signature seasonings. This is one such dish.

In a large sauté pan, melt the ghee over medium heat and sauté the onion for about 10 minutes, or until lightly browned. Add the ginger and cook for 2 minutes longer.

Transfer the mixture to a 7-quart slow cooker and add the tomatoes, cumin, mustard seed, and cinnamon. Cover and cook on LOW for about 4 hours longer.

Just before serving, use a garlic press to mince the garlic into the soup, and add the salt to taste. Using a handheld immersion blender, puree the soup to the desired texture. I like to leave some texture.

Ladle the soup into bowls. Garnish each with cilantro, coconut, and a sprinkling of chile.

2 tablespoons ghee or butter (see page xv)

1 medium onion, chopped

1½-inch piece fresh ginger, peeled and finely chopped

6 large tomatoes, quartered and stemmed

1 teaspoon cumin seed

1 teaspoon black mustard seed

¼ teaspoon ground cinnamon

2 cloves garlic, chopped

Salt

¼ cup chopped fresh cilantro

¼ cup unsweetened shredded coconut

½ serrano chile, seeded and minced

Spiced Lima Bean, Spinach, and Basmati Rice Soup

Serves 4 to 6

2 tablespoons ghee or
    butter (see page xv)

½ medium onion, chopped

1 cup dried lima beans

¼ cup uncooked brown
    basmati rice

½ teaspoon mustard seed

½ teaspoon ground
    turmeric

½ teaspoon ground
    coriander seed

1 cup sliced carrots

6 cups water

3 ounces fresh spinach

¼ cup chopped fresh dill

Salt

¼ cup Greek-style yogurt
    or sour cream

Here is a lima bean soup with an Indian twist to it. This combination of rice and limas provides a source of complete protein and is easy to make. In case you hadn't noticed, I love to juxtapose the textures, colors, and flavors of cooked ingredients with raw. Doing so makes for a more interesting dish. It makes me feel as if I am getting something that is nourishing (because it is hot) and very healthful and exciting (the raw, crunchy stuff).

In a large sauté pan, melt the ghee over medium heat and sauté the onion for about 10 minutes, or until lightly browned.

Transfer the onion to a 7-quart slow cooker and add the beans, rice, mustard seed, turmeric, coriander, carrots, and water. Cover and cook on LOW for about 6 hours, or until the beans are tender.

Stir in the spinach and dill and add the salt to taste.

Ladle the soup into bowls. Serve each with a dollop of yogurt.

Dried Mushroom Barley Soup with Dilled Cream

Serves 4 to 6

Although most Americans have tasted barley only in soup, it bears an honorable place in the survival and proliferation of mankind. Its natural range runs all the way from Crete in the west to Tibet in the east—quite some range, wouldn't you say? And even today it remains the dietary mainstay of the Tibetan people. It has been used to make beer, spirits, flour, and bread, aside from its more common use in soups and stews. I love the way barley feels in my mouth. Those little grains with their slightly resistant texture, swimming around in a nice, rich, and in this case, mushroomy broth, are the perfect thing for a cold night or a rainy day.

In a large sauté pan, heat the oil over medium heat and sauté the onion for about 10 minutes, or until lightly browned. Add the barley, carrots, and celery and cook for 5 minutes longer.

Transfer the mixture to a 7-quart slow cooker and add the mushrooms, bay leaf, seasoning sauce, and water. Cover and cook on LOW for about 6 hours, or until the barley is tender. Add the salt and pepper to taste.

Ladle the soup into bowls and top each with yogurt and a generous sprinkling of dill.

3 tablespoons vegetable oil, butter, or ghee (see page xv)

1 medium onion, thinly sliced

½ cup uncooked barley

1 cup diced carrots

½ cup diced celery

2 ounces dried mushrooms

1 bay leaf

1 tablespoon Maggi Seasoning sauce (see page xiv)

6 cups water

Salt and freshly ground black pepper

½ cup Greek-style yogurt or sour cream

¼ cup chopped fresh dill

Mexican Tomato–Chile Soup with Orange Juice and Zest

Serves 4 to 6

4 dried California or New Mexico chiles, seeded and torn into bits

1 cup water

1 medium white onion, chopped

6 large tomatoes, quartered

1 cup freshly squeezed orange or tangelo juice

4 cloves garlic, or more

Salt

¼ cup fresh cilantro leaves

2 scallions

¼ cup crumbled feta or queso fresco

Grated zest of 1 orange

Mexican dishes often feature various combinations of chile with citrus juice added at the last minute. This is a tomatoey picante soup that will appeal to those who love bold flavors. I pass it around when anyone in my house has a cold, as I view its fresh flavors, dash of garlic, and vitamin C content as good medicine. I would suggest serving it with a quesadilla filled with smoked Gouda or queso fresco and vegetables—sort of the Mexican equivalent of tomato soup with toasted cheese sandwiches.

In a large measuring cup or bowl, soak the chiles in the water for about 2 hours or overnight, or until soft. Puree in a blender until smooth.

Place the chile puree, onion, and tomatoes in a 7-quart slow cooker. Cover and cook on LOW for about 4 hours, or until the tomatoes and onion are quite soft.

Add the orange juice and, using a garlic press, mince the garlic into the soup. Using a handheld immersion blender, puree the ingredients to the desired texture. Add the salt to taste.

Ladle the soup into bowls and top each with cilantro, scallions, cheese, and a sprinkle of orange zest.

Spanish Mushroom–Potato Soup with Pimentón

Serves 4 to 6

Pimentón is one of Spain's most interesting agricultural products, and its smoky flavor is characteristically found in many Spanish dishes. The combination of smoky paprika, potatoes, and mushrooms gives this soup a decidedly earthy, warming flavor.

In a large sauté pan, heat the olive oil over medium heat and sauté the onion for about 10 minutes, or until lightly browned. Add the garlic and cook for 2 minutes longer.

Transfer the mixture to a 7-quart slow cooker and add the mushrooms and potatoes. Cover and cook on LOW (without the water) for about 2 hours.

Add the water and cook for 2 to 3 hours longer, until the potatoes are quite tender. Stir in the paprika and add the salt to taste.

Ladle the soup into bowls and top each with a dollop of crème fraîche.

3 tablespoons olive oil

1 medium onion, halved and thinly sliced

4 cloves garlic, sliced

1 ounce dried porcini mushrooms (preferably Aromatica Organics)

2 large russet potatoes, peeled and chopped

6 cups water

1 tablespoon Spanish smoked paprika (pimentón)

Salt (preferably smoked salt)

6 to 8 tablespoons crème fraîche, sour cream, or Greek-style yogurt

Minestrone

Serves 6 to 8

Unarguably, this is one of Italy's most famous staple dishes. It's made everywhere, and the ingredients vary from season to season and region to region, as well as from cook to cook. Feel free to improvise—this is just a good starting point for Italian comfort food. Although it's not traditionally done this way, I like adding the herbs and garlic near the end of the cooking time so that they remain fresh and alive in taste.

In a large sauté pan, heat the olive oil over medium heat and sauté the onion for about 10 minutes, or until lightly browned.

Rinse the beans thoroughly and add them to the slow cooker along with the onion, tomatoes, Parmesan rind, bay leaf, and water. Cover and cook on LOW for 6 to 8 hours, until the beans are tender.

Add the celery, potato, carrots, and spinach, and salt to taste. Cook for 1 to 2 hours longer, until the potato is tender. Stir in the rosemary and sage. Using a garlic press, mince the garlic into the soup.

Ladle the soup into bowls and top each with a generous sprinkling of Parmesan cheese.

2 tablespoons olive oil

1 medium onion, chopped

1 cup dried cannellini beans or great northern beans

1 (28-ounce) can crushed tomatoes

Parmesan cheese rind

1 bay leaf

5 cups water

3 celery ribs, with leaves

1 medium potato, peeled and diced

2 medium carrots, peeled and diced

1 cup fresh spinach or chard, sliced and loosely packed

Salt

Leaves from 1 sprig fresh rosemary, chopped

3 fresh sage leaves, chopped

3 cloves garlic

½ cup freshly grated Parmesan cheese

New Potato and Parsley Soup with Olive Tapenade

Serves 4 to 6

2 tablespoons butter or ghee (see page xv)

1 medium onion, chopped

1½ pounds small new or red potatoes, skins on

5 cups water

½ cup sour cream

Salt

2 cloves garlic

1 cup chopped fresh parsley

Freshly ground black pepper

¼ cup black or green olive tapenade

Many years ago, my mother and father gave me a Junior League of San Francisco cookbook for Christmas. There I found a simple recipe for delicious potato and parsley soup. Tarragon, dill, or even a combination of herbs would work just as well as, or in addition to, the parsley. Be sure to use organic potatoes since you will be leaving the skins on.

In a large sauté pan, melt the butter over medium heat and sauté the onion for about 10 minutes, or until lightly browned.

Transfer the onion to a 7-quart slow cooker and add the potatoes (without the water). Cover and cook on LOW for about 4 hours, or until the potatoes are quite tender.

Add the water and sour cream and add the salt to taste. Using a garlic press, mince the garlic into the soup. Using a handheld immersion blender, puree some of the soup until the desired texture is reached. I like to leave lots of potato chunks for a rustic appeal.

Cover and cook for 20 to 30 minutes longer, just long enough to heat through. Just before serving, stir in the parsley and add the pepper to taste.

Ladle the soup into bowls and garnish with tapenade.

Potato, Broccoli, and Cheese Soup

Serves 4 to 6

2 tablespoons ghee or
   butter (see page xv)

½ medium onion, coarsely
   chopped

1 large potato, quartered

6 cups water

1 small head broccoli,
   quartered

1 cup grated sharp cheddar
   cheese

Salt

½ cup cream or sour cream

Many years ago when I was a student, a little restaurant called Beggar's Banquet opened a few blocks away from my home. I loved it for no other reason than they made great soups, unlike any I had ever tasted at my mother's table. They were sort of French-style, all creamy and full of fresh vegetable flavor. Several years later, someone who knew the owners told me they were simply giving the previous day's vegetables a whirl in the blender with a dash of cream. So simple, yet so warming and delicious.

In a large sauté pan, melt the ghee over medium heat and sauté the onion for about 10 minutes, or until lightly browned.

Transfer the onion to a 7-quart slow cooker and add the potato and water. Cover and cook on LOW for about 6 hours, or until the potato is quite tender. Add the broccoli during the last 30 minutes of cooking.

Using a handheld immersion blender, puree the ingredients to the desired texture. Stir in the cheese and add the salt to taste.

Ladle the soup into bowls and garnish each with cream.

Potato, Cheese, and Asparagus Soup

Serves 4 to 6

If you want to coax extra flavor out of any soup based upon potatoes, onions, or other root vegetables, first cook the potatoes and onions in the slow cooker without the water for a couple of hours to allow for some browning and to give the flavors a chance to develop. After a couple of hours, you can add the liquid and continue to finish cooking the soup. If you are pressed for time, you can add the water when you add the potatoes.

In a large sauté pan, heat the vegetable oil over medium heat and sauté the onion for about 10 minutes, or until lightly browned. Add the garlic and cook for 2 minutes longer.

Transfer the mixture to a 7-quart slow cooker and add the potatoes (without the water). Cover and cook on LOW for about 6 hours, or until the potatoes are quite tender.

Add the water, and using a handheld immersion blender, puree the mixture until smooth. Add the nutmeg and salt and pepper to taste. Add the asparagus and cook for 15 to 30 minutes longer, until the asparagus spears are just tender.

Ladle the soup into bowls. Serve hot, sprinkled with 1 to 2 tablespoons cheddar cheese.

2 tablespoons vegetable oil or butter

1 medium onion, coarsely chopped

3 cloves garlic, coarsely chopped

2 large russet potatoes, peeled and sliced into fat rounds

6 cups water

Dash of freshly grated nutmeg

Salt (preferably smoked) and freshly ground black pepper

12 young asparagus spears, cut into ½-inch pieces, rough ends removed

½ cup grated sharp cheddar cheese

Spanish Potato and Green Olive Soup

Serves 4 to 6

4 tablespoons olive oil, divided

1 medium onion, chopped

1½ pounds small potatoes

1 bay leaf

2 sprigs fresh thyme

6 cups water

1½ cups stuffed green olives, sliced in half vertically

Salt

1 cup cubed Manchego or cheddar cheese

This recipe was inspired by a soup served at a winery in Toro, Spain. Serve with a crusty loaf of French bread and perhaps a hearty red Tinta de Toro (the local name for the Tempranillo grape) from Toro.

In a large sauté pan, heat 2 tablespoons of the olive oil over medium heat and sauté the onion for about 10 minutes, or until lightly browned.

Transfer the onion to a 7-quart slow cooker and add the potatoes, bay leaf, and thyme. Cover and cook on LOW (without the water) for about 4 hours, or until the potatoes are tender.

Add the water and, using a fork or potato masher, smash the potatoes. If you prefer a smooth texture, you can use an immersion blender to puree them.

Stir in the olives and add the salt to taste. Continue cooking for 30 to 40 minutes longer, until the soup is once again hot.

To serve, divide the cheese into bowls, drizzle the remaining olive oil over it, then ladle in the soup and stir.

Pasta e Fagioli

Serves 4 to 6

2 tablespoons olive oil

1 medium onion, chopped

4 large cloves garlic, finely chopped

1 cup dried borlotti (cranberry) beans

5 cups water

2 medium carrots, sliced

2 celery ribs, sliced

Parmesan cheese rinds

1 (8-ounce) can tomato sauce

½ cup uncooked ditalini or other small tubular pasta

Salt

¼ cup freshly grated Parmesan cheese

¼ cup chopped fresh parsley (see Note)

Also known as "pasta fazool," this is another rustic Italian favorite, and like minestrone and ribollita, its contents may vary from season to season, region to region, and cook to cook. Perhaps the main difference between pasta e fagioli (which means "pasta and beans") and the other classic Italian soups is the addition of pasta. While ditalini or small elbow macaroni are traditional, there are many other interesting types of pasta that would also work well. Borlotti (cranberry) beans are also traditional, but I've made this soup using pinquitos, white beans, and a 10-bean mixture, all with good results. Use as many Parmesan cheese rinds as you'd like.

In a sauté pan, heat the olive oil over medium heat and sauté the onion for about 10 minutes, or until lightly browned. Add the garlic and cook for 2 minutes longer.

Transfer the mixture to a 7-quart slow cooker and add the beans, water, carrots, celery, Parmesan rinds, and tomato sauce. Cover and cook on LOW for about 6 hours, or until the beans are tender.

About 1 hour before serving, stir in the ditalini and add the salt to taste. Cook for about 1 hour, or until the ditalini is cooked al dente.

Ladle your soup into bowls and serve each with a dusting of Parmesan cheese and a sprinkle of parsley.

Note: A typical Italian finish for a soup is to drizzle fruity olive oil over the top of each serving at the table. You could do that instead of or in addition to the parsley and Parmesan.

Soupe au Pistou

Serves 4 to 6

2 tablespoons olive oil

1 medium yellow onion, coarsely chopped

1 medium eggplant, peeled and cut into chunks

1 Parmesan cheese rind (optional)

6 cups water

1 medium zucchini, cut into 1-inch cubes

1 medium green bell pepper, cut into 1-inch pieces

2 large tomatoes, coarsely chopped

1 cup Mediterranean-style olives, halved

1 sprig fresh thyme

1 to 2 sprigs fresh basil

Salt and freshly ground black pepper

This soup contains all the delicious flavors commonly found in the summer dishes of southern France and Italy: basil, eggplant, garlic, tomatoes, and zucchini. The vegetables give it a hearty base, and the pistou—a classic finish for Provençal dishes (akin to Italian pesto)—gives a burst of flavor that gets swirled in just before serving. Best recommendation of all? Make this soup with vegetables straight from your summer garden.

In a large sauté pan, heat the olive oil over medium heat and sauté the onion for about 10 minutes, or until lightly browned.

Transfer the onion to a 7-quart slow cooker and add the eggplant, Parmesan rind, and water. Cover and cook on LOW for about 4 hours, or until the eggplant is quite tender.

Add the zucchini, bell pepper, tomatoes, olives, thyme, and basil and cook for 1 hour longer, or until the vegetables are soft.

Remove the Parmesan rind and the sprigs of thyme and basil from the soup, then add the salt and pepper to taste.

To make the pistou, place the basil, Parmesan cheese, and garlic in the work bowl of a food processor and let it run until the basil and garlic are finely chopped. Turn off the machine and scrape down the sides of the bowl, then turn the machine back on, and drizzle the olive oil slowly through the feed tube, letting it run until smooth. Add the salt to taste.

Ladle the soup into bowls. To serve, drizzle some of the pistou over the top of each bowl and sprinkle with Parmesan cheese.

Pistou

**2 cups tightly packed fresh
   basil leaves**

**½ cup freshly grated
   Parmesan cheese**

3 large cloves garlic

¼ cup olive oil

Salt

**¼ cup freshly grated
   Parmesan cheese**

Real Cream of Tomato Soup

Serves 4 to 6

2 to 3 pounds tomatoes (homegrown, if possible), quartered

½ medium onion, coarsely chopped

1 to 2 cloves garlic

1 cup cream

Salt

Chile flakes (optional)

4 basil leaves, cut into chiffonade (see page 14)

Practically every person I know ate Campbell's Tomato Soup with grilled cheese sandwiches when they were a kid. Even Oprah. You might think of this recipe as cream of tomato soup gone uptown. It is simple and delicious, especially when made with tomatoes straight from your garden. For a little more kick, add some chile flakes.

Place the tomatoes, onion, and garlic in a 7-quart slow cooker. Cover and cook on LOW for 3 to 4 hours, until the tomatoes are soft and falling apart.

Using a handheld immersion blender, puree the mixture until the desired texture is achieved. Stir in the cream and add the salt to taste. If needed, you can add some water, but this will most likely not be necessary. Add the chile flakes to taste.

Ladle the soup into bowls and garnish each bowl with the basil.

Red Posole

Serves 4 to 6

2 cups dried posole

6 cups water

2 tablespoons vegetable oil

1 medium white onion, chopped

2 teaspoons ground cumin seed

1 teaspoon coriander seed

2 tablespoons chile powder

2 teaspoons dried Mexican oregano

4 cloves garlic, minced

1 (14.5-ounce) can diced tomatoes (optional)

Juice of ½ lime

Salt

Posole (or pozole) is both an ingredient and a soup that can be found in Mexican restaurants and on tables across the Southwest. Its characteristic ingredient is posole (hominy), dried field corn that has been soaked in lime to loosen its tough skin, which is then removed. (This is the same process used to render field corn suitable for making tamales and tortillas.) You can use canned hominy in a pinch (and your cooking time will be greatly shortened), but good quality dried posole will yield a much more satisfying flavor and texture. I order white posole from the Santa Fe School of Cooking's online market in order to avoid the hassle of trying to find good quality posole locally with its skin already removed. Posole (the soup) can be red or green, depending upon what color chiles you use.

Rinse the dried posole thoroughly, then place it in a 7-quart slow cooker along with the water. Cover and cook on LOW for about 6 hours, or until the posole kernels are beginning to burst open.

While the posole is cooking, heat the oil in a large sauté pan over medium heat and sauté the onion for about 10 minutes, or until lightly browned.

Crush the cumin and coriander seeds in a mortar and pestle or grind it in a spice grinder. Add the cumin, coriander, chile powder, oregano, garlic, and tomatoes to the onion and cook for 2 to 3 minutes longer.

Add the mixture to the slow cooker and continue cooking for 1 to 2 hours longer, until the flavors meld. Stir in the lime juice and add the salt to taste. (Posole requires a lot of salt, so don't be stingy.)

Ladle the posole into bowls. Serve with assorted garnishes so that people can add their own toppings.

Garnishes

Chopped fresh cilantro

Sliced radishes

Shredded napa cabbage

Sliced black olives

Chopped white onion

Diced avocado

Crumbled Cotija or feta cheese

Sour cream

Lime wedges

Red Pepper Soup with Basil Chiffonade

Serves 4 to 6

2 tablespoons olive oil or ghee (see page xv)

1 medium onion, coarsely chopped

2 cloves garlic

1 bay leaf

4 large red bell peppers, seeded, and thickly sliced or chopped

2 medium carrots, peeled and sliced

1 large tomato, coarsely chopped

5 cups water

1 cup half-and-half

Salt

½ cup sour cream

4 basil leaves, cut into chiffonade (see page 14)

This is a luscious, bright red soup, but to fully realize the bell pepper flavor, I recommend serving it the day after you make it. I find the bell pepper flavor is quite faint when the soup is freshly made (one neighbor couldn't even detect the bell pepper flavor), but after it stands overnight, the flavor ripens and the soup blossoms. Serve it hot or cold, topped with a dollop of sour cream and a sprinkling of basil chiffonade.

In a large sauté pan, heat the oil over medium heat and sauté the onion for about 10 minutes, or until lightly browned. Add the garlic and cook for 1 to 2 minutes longer. Do not let the garlic brown.

Transfer the mixture to a 7-quart slow cooker and add the bay leaf, bell peppers, carrots, and tomato. Cover and cook on LOW for about 4 hours, or until the peppers and carrots are tender.

Add the water, then using a handheld blender, puree the contents of the slow cooker until the desired texture has been reached. Stir in the half-and-half and add the salt to taste.

Ladle the soup into bowls and top each with a dollop of sour cream and some basil.

Ribollita

Serves 4 to 6

I wrote all the recipes for this book one winter. How perfect—all that cold weather, and all of those great, hot soup experiments. In my close-knit neighborhood, everyone wanted in on the kitchen magic. Like minestrone, ribollita is an Italian (Tuscan) classic, and its name means "reboiled." It was originally made by reboiling yesterday's minestrone. Same basic soup, different day.

In a large sauté pan, heat the olive oil over medium heat and sauté the onion for about 10 minutes, or until lightly browned. Add the garlic and cook for 2 minutes longer.

Transfer the mixture to a 7-quart slow cooker and add the water, beans, Parmesan rind, tomato paste, celery, and carrots. Cover and cook on LOW for about 8 hours, or until the beans are tender.

Thirty minutes before serving, stir in the chard, cabbage, and zucchini. Add the salt to taste and continue cooking until the zucchini is tender. Stir in the vinegar.

Ladle the soup into bowls and top each with a sprinkling of parsley and Parmesan cheese.

2 tablespoons olive oil

1 medium onion, cut into 10 pieces

6 cloves garlic, sliced

6 cups water

1 cup dried cannellini or other white beans

Parmesan cheese rind

1 tablespoon tomato paste

3 celery ribs, sliced

2 medium carrots, sliced

1 cup sliced chard

1 cup sliced napa cabbage

1 medium zucchini, diced

Salt

¼ cup white vinegar

½ cup chopped fresh parsley

½ cup freshly grated Parmesan cheese

Swedish Rhubarb Raspberry Soup

Serves 4 to 6

2 pounds fresh or frozen
    sliced rhubarb

6 cups water

1 cup granulated sugar

1 (10-ounce) package frozen
    raspberries

½ cup sour cream or
    whipped cream

Honey, for drizzling

Ground cinnamon, for
    sprinkling

I have always been a rhubarb hound. I love its tart, fruity flavor, and as a child, I remember clamoring for my mom to make rhubarb pie; the more tart, the better. It was my favorite thing. I have since found a number of different ways to enjoy rhubarb, among them a traditional Norwegian rhubarb soup. It can be served hot, warm, or cold. And should you have any left over, you can use it as a sauce over yogurt or ice cream, or use it as a base for a delicious smoothie. You can add cinnamon if you like, but I am a purist and prefer the unadulterated rhubarb flavor. The dish is especially beautiful when served either in clear glass or white porcelain bowls.

Place the rhubarb, water, and sugar in a 7-quart slow cooker. Cover and cook on LOW for about 6 hours, or until the rhubarb has "melted."

Using a handheld immersion blender, puree some or all of the rhubarb to your preferred texture. Add the raspberries and cook for 30 minutes longer, or until the soup is once again hot.

Serve the soup warm in bowls topped with a tablespoon of sour cream or whipped cream, a drizzle of honey, and a sprinkle of cinnamon.

Sopa de Ajo

Serves 4 to 6

¼ **cup olive oil**

1 medium onion, coarsely chopped

4 large heads garlic, cloves separated and peeled

6 cups water

Juice of 1 lemon

Salt

1 ripe avocado, diced

4 ounces queso fresco or feta, crumbled

1 medium firm tomato, diced

1 bunch cilantro, stems removed

¼ **cup sliced scallions**

There is a Mexican restaurant in my town that specializes in caldos, or Mexican broth-based soups. Everyone goes there to get caldo on a cold day, but everyone especially goes there for take-out caldo when they feel a cold or flu coming on. All that garlic and hot broth clears the head—even if you don't have a cold.

Place the oil, onion, and garlic in the slow cooker. Cover and cook on LOW for about 6 hours or until the garlic is quite tender.

Add the water and cook for 2 hours. Using a handheld immersion blender, puree the soup. Add the lemon juice, then add the salt to taste.

To serve, place some of the avocado, cheese, and tomato in the bottom of each bowl, then ladle in the broth over the ingredients. Top each bowl with a sprinkle of cilantro and some scallions.

Spiced Spinach Dal with Coconut Milk

Serves 4 to 6

In southern India, dal is soupy and served over rice; in northern India, dal is a thicker consistency for scooping up with roti, the traditional Indian wheat flatbread. You can vary the amount of water in this recipe in accordance with whether you want a proper soup or a more stewlike consistency.

In a large sauté pan, heat the oil over medium heat and sauté the onion for about 10 minutes, or until lightly brown. Add the garlic and cook for 1 to 2 minutes longer.

Rinse the lentils thoroughly and place them in a 7-quart slow cooker along with the onion and garlic mixture and the water.

Using a spice grinder or mortar and pestle, grind the cumin and coriander seeds to a powder, then add them, along with the turmeric, cardamom, and cinnamon to the lentils. Cover and cook on LOW for 4 to 6 hours, until the lentils are quite tender.

Stir in the coconut milk and spinach, and add the salt to taste. Cook for 20 minutes longer, or until the soup is once again hot and all the spinach is wilted.

Ladle the soup into bowls. Top each with a bit of chopped chile, a sprinkle of cilantro, and some coconut.

2 tablespoons ghee or oil (see page xv)

1 medium onion, chopped

4 cloves garlic, slivered

1 cup dried yellow lentils

4 cups water

1 teaspoon cumin seed

1 teaspoon coriander seed

1 teaspoon ground turmeric

½ teaspoon ground cardamom

1 teaspoon ground cinnamon

1 (15-ounce) can coconut milk

4 ounces fresh spinach

Salt

1 serrano chile, seeded and finely diced

2 tablespoons chopped fresh cilantro

¼ cup shredded coconut, toasted

Spiced Apple Pie Soup

Serves 4 to 6

1 stick cinnamon

6 cloves

6 allspice berries

4 tablespoons (½ stick)
unsalted butter, melted

5 large Granny Smith
apples, quartered, cored,
and sliced

5 cups water

⅔ cup raisins

1 tablespoon freshly
squeezed lemon juice
(optional)

3 to 4 tablespoons honey
(optional)

½ cup Greek-style yogurt
or sour cream

If you've got a burning desire to keep 'em down on the farm during the fall or winter holiday season, here's the perfect way to do it. Fill the house with the smell of spiced apples. I recommend using Granny Smith apples, as most other apple varieties are likely to produce a weaker version of this soup. You need acid and flavor, and the Granny Smith delivers both. Try to find organic apples, then leave the skins intact as most of the flavor and nutrients are found in or just under the skins of the fruit. Use your imagination when it comes to garnishes: perhaps some chopped, toasted walnuts, grated sharp cheddar cheese, or a dollop of sour cream or yogurt.

Using a spice grinder or mortar and pestle, grind the cinnamon, cloves, and allspice to a fine powder.

Place the butter and apples in a 7-quart slow cooker. Cover and cook on LOW for 2 to 3 hours, until the apples are soft and the juice nice and browned. Mash any large pieces of apple, then add the water, spices, and raisins and continue cooking for 2 hours longer.

Just before serving, stir in the lemon juice and honey.

To serve, ladle the soup into bowls and top with the yogurt.

Spring Red Plum Soup

Serves 4 to 6

This is another simple yet thoroughly delicious recipe. I use red plums because I find them to be more flavorful than other plums—especially their skins, where most of the flavor and tartness lie. I think any good plum would work, however. This soup can be served either hot with nothing other than the full, rich flavor of plums to savor, or cold topped with yogurt. I often eat the leftovers cold spooned over a bowl of yogurt or cereal for breakfast.

2 pounds red plums

2 cups water

1 tablespoon apple pie spice

$\frac{1}{4}$ to $\frac{1}{2}$ cup granulated sugar

1 cup freshly squeezed orange juice

$\frac{1}{2}$ cup yogurt or crème fraîche

Quarter the plums and remove their pits. Place them and the water in a 7-quart slow cooker. Cover and cook on LOW for 4 hours or until the plums are falling apart.

Smash the plums with the back of a spoon, then add the apple pie spice, sugar, and orange juice. Mix thoroughly.

Ladle the soup into bowls and top with the yogurt or crème fraîche.

Tuscan White Bean Soup with Olive Oil and Rosemary

Serves 4 to 6

2 cups dried white beans, such as great northern or cannellini

6 cups water

1 medium onion, chopped

6 cloves garlic

1 bay leaf

Salt

¼ cup olive oil

1 tablespoon chopped fresh rosemary

One of the things I love about the cooking of rural Italy is its simplicity. A simple dish of pasta with tomato and herb sauce. A simple loaf of bread. A rustic wine. The cook is not required to rummage through pantries, or multiple grocery stores and ethnic markets, looking for ingredients. Often she may look no further than her own garden or local farmers' market. Puree the beans or eat them whole, as you wish.

Rinse the beans thoroughly and place them in a 7-quart slow cooker along with the water, onion, garlic, and bay leaf. Cover and cook on LOW for about 8 hours, or until the beans are nice and tender.

Remove the bay leaf. Using a handheld immersion blender, puree the remaining ingredients to the desired texture. Add the salt to taste.

Ladle the soup into bowls. Drizzle with the olive oil, sprinkle with rosemary, and serve.

Waters Mulligatawny Soup

Serves 4 to 6

1 cup dried chickpeas (garbanzo beans)

¼ cup uncooked brown rice

1 medium onion, chopped

2 cloves garlic, finely minced

6 cups water

1 tablespoon curry powder

1 (14-ounce) can coconut cream

½ cup raisins

Salt

1 large Granny Smith apple, cored and finely diced

½ cup chopped walnuts

½ cup grated smoked Gouda or cheddar cheese

¼ cup chopped fresh cilantro

¼ cup pomegranate seeds (optional)

My friend Andrew Spurgin is the executive director of Waters Fine Catering in San Diego. Each day, Waters takeout shop offers a different homemade soup. Their mulligatawny, a classic from the days of the British occupation of India, is one of my favorites. Although traditionally made with chicken and chicken stock, I thought I'd try creating a version from the basics alone. The neighbors lined up at the door with bowls in hand. I like using the apple, walnuts, cilantro, and pomegranate as condiments rather than cooking them in the soup. It adds a fresh note to the composition. And although it is not typically Indian, I also love adding a bit of grated very sharp cheddar cheese.

Rinse the chickpeas and rice thoroughly and place them in a 7-quart slow cooker along with the onion, garlic, and water. Cover and cook on LOW for 6 to 8 hours, until the chickpeas are tender.

Using a handheld immersion blender, puree just a few of the chickpeas to add some thickness to the soup, then add the curry powder, coconut cream, and raisins. Add the salt to taste. Cook for 20 to 30 minutes longer, or until nice and hot.

Top each bowl of soup with the apple, walnuts, cheese, cilantro, and pomegranate seeds.

White Miso Winter Soup

Serves 4 to 6

Miso is a traditional Japanese seasoning made with fermented soy, wheat, barley, or rice, or any combination of the above. The textures, flavors, and appearance of traditional miso varies from region to region in Japan. The most typical types of miso found in the Western world are red and white miso used as a base for soups or a seasoning for Japanese dishes. This plain miso soup is enlivened with typical winter vegetables.

Place the water, onion, carrots, and squash in a 7-quart slow cooker. Cover and cook on LOW for about 4 hours, or until the vegetables are tender.

About 20 minutes before serving, add the broccoli florets and the miso and cook until just tender. Just before serving, finely grate the ginger into the soup.

Ladle the soup into bowls. Top each serving with the sliced scallions and a drizzle of sesame oil.

6 cups water

1 medium onion, sliced into 8 pieces from pole to pole

2 medium carrots, peeled and sliced

½ small butternut squash, peeled and cubed

¾ cup small broccoli florets

2 tablespoons white miso

½-inch piece fresh ginger, peeled

2 scallions, thinly sliced

2 tablespoons toasted sesame oil

Metric Conversions and Equivalents

Metric Conversion Formulas

To Convert	Multiply
Ounces to grams	Ounces by 28.35
Pounds to kilograms	Pounds by .454
Teaspoons to milliliters	Teaspoons by 4.93
Tablespoons to milliliters	Tablespoons by 14.79
Fluid ounces to milliliters	Fluid ounces by 29.57
Cups to milliliters	Cups by 236.59
Cups to liters	Cups by .236
Pints to liters	Pints by .473
Quarts to liters	Quarts by .946
Gallons to liters	Gallons by 3.785
Inches to centimeters	Inches by 2.54

Approximate Metric Equivalents

Volume

¼ teaspoon	1 milliliter
½ teaspoon	2.5 milliliters
¾ teaspoon	4 milliliters
1 teaspoon	5 milliliters
1¼ teaspoons	6 milliliters
1½ teaspoons	7.5 milliliters
1¾ teaspoons	8.5 milliliters
2 teaspoons	10 milliliters
1 tablespoon (½ fluid ounce)	15 milliliters
2 tablespoons (1 fluid ounce)	30 milliliters
¼ cup	60 milliliters
⅓ cup	80 milliliters
½ cup (4 fluid ounces)	120 milliliters
⅔ cup	160 milliliters
¾ cup	180 milliliters
1 cup (8 fluid ounces)	240 milliliters
1¼ cups	300 milliliters
1½ cups (12 fluid ounces)	360 milliliters
1⅔ cups	400 milliliters
2 cups (1 pint)	460 milliliters
3 cups	700 milliliters
4 cups (1 quart)	.95 liter
1 quart plus ¼ cup	1 liter
4 quarts (1 gallon)	3.8 liters

Weight

¼ ounce	7 grams
½ ounce	14 grams
¾ ounce	21 grams
1 ounce	28 grams
1¼ ounces	35 grams
1½ ounces	42.5 grams
1⅔ ounces	45 grams
2 ounces	57 grams
3 ounces	85 grams
4 ounces (¼ pound)	113 grams
5 ounces	142 grams
6 ounces	170 grams
7 ounces	198 grams
8 ounces (½ pound)	227 grams
16 ounces (1 pound)	454 grams
35.25 ounces (2.2 pounds)	1 kilogram

Length

⅛ inch	3 millimeters
¼ inch	6 millimeters
½ inch	1¼ centimeters
1 inch	2½ centimeters
2 inches	5 centimeters
2½ inches	6 centimeters

4 inches	10 centimeters
5 inches	13 centimeters
6 inches	15¼ centimeters
12 inches (1 foot)	30 centimeters

Oven Temperatures

To convert Fahrenheit to Celsius, subtract 32 from Fahrenheit, multiply the result by 5, then divide by 9.

Description	Fahrenheit	Celsius	British Gas Mark
Very cool	200°	95°	0
Very cool	225°	110°	¼
Very cool	250°	120°	½
Cool	275°	135°	1
Cool	300°	150°	2
Warm	325°	165°	3
Moderate	350°	175°	4
Moderately hot	375°	190°	5
Fairly hot	400°	200°	6
Hot	425°	220°	7
Very hot	450°	230°	8
Very hot	475°	245°	9

Common Ingredients and Their Approximate Equivalents

1 cup uncooked rice = 225 grams
1 cup all-purpose flour = 140 grams
1 stick butter (4 ounces • ½ cup • 8 tablespoons) = 110 grams
1 cup butter (8 ounces • 2 sticks • 16 tablespoons) = 220 grams
1 cup brown sugar, firmly packed = 225 grams
1 cup granulated sugar = 200 grams

Information compiled from a variety of sources, including *Recipes into Type* by Joan Whitman and Dolores Simon (Newton, MA: Biscuit Books, 2000); *The New Food Lover's Companion* by Sharon Tyler Herbst (Hauppauge, NY: Barron's, 1995); and *Rosemary Brown's Big Kitchen Instruction Book* (Kansas City, MO: Andrews McMeel, 1998).

Index